BEFORE THEY WERE FAMOUS

FAMOUS

HOW SEVEN ARTISTS GOT THEIR START

BOB
RACZKA

M MILLBROOK PRESS / MINNEAPOLIS

To every kid who loves to draw—the artists of tomorrow

Text copyright © 2011 by Bob Raczka

Millbrook Press
A division of Lerner Publishing Group, Inc.
241 First Avenue North
Minneapolis, MN 55401 U.S.A.

Website address: www.lernerbooks.com

Library of Congress Cataloging-in-Publication Data

Raczka, Bob.
    Before they were famous : how seven artists got their start / by Bob Raczka.
        p.   cm.
    ISBN: 978-0-7613-6077-3 (lib. bdg. : alk. paper)
    1. Child artists. 2. Young artists. 3. Creative ability in children. 4. Creative ability in adolescence. I. Title. II. Title: How seven artists got their start.
    N351.R33 2011
    704'.083—dc22   2009049596

Manufactured in the United States of America
1 – DP – 7/15/10

INTRODUCTION

One day, in a book I was reading, I came across an interesting painting of a man on a horse (see page 25). The man was dressed in yellow, his horse was brown, and they were in some sort of arena where people were watching them. The painting was done by the famous Spanish artist Pablo Picasso—when he was eight!

I was fascinated. I could tell that even as a young boy, Pablo was talented. I wondered if I could find early paintings or drawings from other famous artists. That's how the idea for this book was born.

It wasn't easy, but I found the childhood artwork of seven different artists. Six were men, and one was a woman. Three grew up over three hundred years ago, and four grew up in the last two hundred years. Four had artistic parents, and three did not. But all seven had one thing in common: as kids, they loved to draw. So make sure your parents save a few of your favorite art projects. Who knows, maybe you'll grow up to be a famous artist!

ALBRECHTDURER
(May 21, 1471–April 6, 1528)

Did you know that Albrecht Durer's mother had eighteen children, yet only three of them lived past childhood?

Albrecht was lucky. He not only survived, he became one of the greatest artists of his time. Albrecht was born in Nuremberg, a city in modern-day Germany. He probably started drawing when he was three. He went to school for a while, where he learned how to read and write. But at age twelve, Albrecht became an apprentice, or student, of his father, a successful goldsmith.

From his father, Albrecht learned to use engraving tools like the burin. He also learned a detailed drawing technique called silverpoint. He learned well. At age thirteen, Albrecht made an incredibly lifelike self-portrait in silverpoint. At age fifteen, he decided he wanted to be an artist and not a goldsmith.

His father was disappointed that his son would not follow in his footsteps. But he agreed to let Albrecht become an apprentice of Michael Wolgemut. Master Wolgemut was a respected Nuremberg painter. He lived on the same street as the Durers. In Wolgemut's workshop, Albrecht learned important skills, like how to grind and mix oil paints and how to prepare wood panels for painting.

Wolgemut also specialized in making woodcut illustrations. This involves carving drawings into blocks of wood, applying ink to the blocks, and then pressing the blocks onto paper. During Albrecht's three years with Wolgemut, he helped his master create hundreds of woodcut illustrations. Many were for early printed books like *The Nuremberg Chronicle*. In fact, before he became famous as a painter, Albrecht was known as a master of woodcut illustration.

When he was eighteen, Albrecht finished his apprenticeship. He spent the next four years traveling around Germany and the Netherlands. He met other artists, and they shared ideas. Albrecht was always eager to try new things. He was the first artist outside of England to use watercolors. He was the first northern European artist to paint landscapes. He was also the first artist to sign his paintings with a logo he designed himself. It was a small capital *D* under the crossbar of a large capital *A* (see pages 6 and 7).

ALBRECHT
AT **13**

Self-Portrait

1484

Albertina,
Vienna, Austria

Albrecht drew this self-portrait when he was only thirteen years old. It is a silverpoint drawing, made by dragging a silver wire across paper coated with primer. Silverpoint allows an artist to make very thin, precise lines. But once a line is drawn, it cannot be erased. This is the earliest known work by Albrecht. It is also one of the first self-portraits in the history of European art.

Portrait of Father

1490

Uffizi Gallery,
Florence, Italy

This portrait of Albrecht's father is his earliest surviving oil painting.
Albrecht painted it when he was nineteen. He had just finished his apprenticeship to the painter, Michael Wolgemut. It was Albrecht's way of
thanking his father for letting him train as a painter. Later the same year,
he also painted a portrait of his mother.

Throughout his life, Albrecht made watercolor paintings of the places he traveled and the animals he saw. This painting of a young hare is one of his most famous. Albrecht painted it when he was thirty-one. Amazingly, he did not start with a sketch. Albrecht painted it entirely with brushes. The hare was probably stuffed, but this detailed painting is full of life.

ALBRECHT
AT**31**

Young Hare
1502
Albertina,
Vienna, Austria

MICHELANGELO
BUONARROTI
(March 6, 1475–February 18, 1564)

Did you know that Michelangelo often skipped school so he could practice drawing famous works of art?

Michelangelo was born near Florence, Italy. When he was very young, his mother became ill and couldn't care for him. So his father sent him to live on a farm with a family of stonecutters. Their job was to dig marble out of the hillside quarries. This is probably where Michelangelo first learned to use a hammer and chisel, the tools of a sculptor.

Michelangelo's father didn't want him to use his hands to earn a living. He thought trades like painting and sculpting were beneath his family. So when Michelangelo was ten, his father sent him to a grammar school in Florence. There he learned to read and write.

But Michelangelo often skipped school to watch the art apprentices of Florence as they worked. Along the way, he met an older boy named Francesco Granacci. Francesco worked for Domenico Ghirlandaio, the famous Florentine painter. Soon Michelangelo and Francesco were roaming the city together, copying famous works of art.

When Michelangelo was about thirteen, Francesco showed his drawings to Master Ghirlandaio. The painter saw his talent and invited him to become an apprentice. He even convinced Michelangelo's father to give his permission. Michelangelo learned all about painting on walls covered with fresh plaster, called fresco painting. He mixed pigments, made brushes, and prepared the plaster. To improve his drawing skills, he copied the works of earlier well-known artists from Florence, like Giotto and Masaccio.

By the time Michelangelo was fifteen, his work had captured the attention of Lorenzo de Medici, the most powerful man in Florence. He practically adopted Michelangelo, giving him his own room at the Medici Palace. There Michelangelo learned how to sculpt marble from the respected sculptor, Bertoldo di Giovanni. He also met many visiting artists and scholars, who shared their ideas with him.

Unfortunately, de Medici died when Michelangelo was seventeen. Now he had to find his own work as an artist. When he was nineteen, he tried his luck in Bologna. At twenty-one, he moved to Rome, where he began to make his reputation as one of the greatest sculptors who ever lived.

MICHELANGELO
AT 12

The Torment of Saint Anthony
ca. 1487–1488
Kimbell Art Museum,
Fort Worth, Texas

As a boy, Michelangelo was friends with a painter's apprentice named Francesco. One day, when Michelangelo was about twelve, Francesco brought him a scary-looking drawing to copy. It was called *The Torment of Saint Anthony*. Michelangelo carefully drew it onto a piece of wood and then filled it in with his own colors. This is his earliest known painting.

This sculpture is one of the first Michelangelo ever attempted. He did it when he was just seventeen years old. Michelangelo was inspired by *Battle of the Horsemen*, a famous sculpture by his teacher, Bertoldo di Giovanni. Because this piece is not finished, we can see the bodies emerging from the stone. Michelangelo kept this sculpture all his life.

MICHELANGELO
AT 17

Battle of the Centaurs
ca. 1492
Casa Buonarroti,
Florence, Italy

Pietà
1499
Saint Peter's Basilica,
Vatican City

The word *pietà* is Italian for pity. It describes any work of art that shows the Virgin Mary grieving over the body of Jesus. This is the first of four *Pietà*s by Michelangelo, but it's the only one he ever finished. It's also the only sculpture he ever signed. Michelangelo completed it when he was just twenty-four years old. It is his first masterpiece.

ARTEMISIA GENTILESCHI
(July 8, 1593–ca. 1656)

Did you know that when Artemisia Gentileschi was growing up, girls were not allowed to become painters?

Artemisia was born in Rome, Italy. The oldest of four children, Artemisia was the only girl. She was also the only child to become a painter like her father. His painting studio was in their home, and his artist friends were always visiting. Observing the artist's way of life up close made a big impression on her.

Artemisia was lucky to live in Rome, where she was surrounded by great art. Many new churches were being built during this time, and many new works of art were being created to decorate them. While she was growing up, she saw Michelangelo's paintings in the Sistine Chapel. She also saw the work of Caravaggio, another great Italian painter, who knew her father.

About the time she was twelve, Artemisia became an apprentice to her father. This was very unusual. During the 1600s in Europe, women were not allowed to work in trades like painting. The only way Artemisia could become an artist was to be taught by her father.

So between the ages of twelve and seventeen, Artemisia learned as much as she could from him. He taught her how to draw the human body. He taught her how to control light, shade, and color in paint. He even sent her on art "field trips." She traveled by carriage to churches throughout Rome, where she could see new artwork in progress.

By the time she was seventeen, Artemisia had completed her first major painting. It was an incredibly dramatic and realistic scene from the Bible titled *Susanna and the Elders*. When she was nineteen, her father was so proud of her painting accomplishments, he bragged that she had no equal.

About this time, Artemisia left Rome for Florence. Before long, she was painting for the city's powerful Medici family. She also became the first female member of the famous Academy of Drawing in Florence. Artemisia was on her way to making a living from her art. This was an amazing achievement for a woman of her time.

ARTEMISIA
AT**17**

*Saint Cecilia Playing
the Lute*
ca. 1610–1612
Spada Gallery,
Rome, Italy

This is one of Artemisia's earliest works. She painted it between the ages of seventeen and nineteen, when her father was training her. She may have been inspired by her father's painting *Young Woman with a Violin*. Both paintings show women playing stringed instruments. And both women look up with the same dreamy expression on their faces.

ARTEMISIA
AT19

Judith Slaying Holofernes
ca. 1612–1613
Museo di Capodimonte,
Naples, Italy

Artemisia often painted heroic women from religious stories. Here she shows Judith, the Jewish woman who saved her city from an invading army by cutting off the head of its general, Holofernes. Painted when she was nineteen or twenty, this is the most violent work Artemisia ever did. It is very dark and dramatic, which shows that she was influenced by the great Italian painter, Caravaggio.

There are nearly sixty known paintings by Artemisia. More than forty of them feature a woman as the main subject. When she was forty-five, Artemisia painted herself as the allegory, or symbol, of painting. Since women were not supposed to become painters, this was her way of saying to the world that a woman could paint just as well as a man.

ARTEMISIA
AT**45**

Self-Portrait as the Allegory of Painting
ca. 1638—1639
The Royal Collection, Kensington Palace,
London, England

JOHN SINGER SARGENT
(January 12, 1856–April 14, 1925)

Did you know that because he grew up in Europe, John Singer Sargent learned to speak French, Italian, and German as a boy?

John was born in Florence, Italy. His parents were from Philadelphia, Pennsylvania, but they left the United States to live in Europe before he was born. John didn't visit the United States for the first time until he was twenty.

John's parents both had artistic talent. His father was a surgeon. He also published medical textbooks, which he illustrated himself. His mother was an amateur artist who enjoyed sketching and watercolor painting. They both encouraged John to draw at a young age.

John always drew from observation, rather than from his imagination. His earliest surviving drawing is of his father, done when he was four. His parents often included his drawings in letters to relatives in the United States. As he got older, John drew all the places his family traveled. He drew everything from pictures he saw in the newspaper to animals he saw at the zoo.

His family traveled constantly. They lived in Italy, France, Britain, Spain, Switzerland, and Germany. As a result, John had few friends and had to entertain himself. He read a lot and learned to play the piano and the mandolin. His mother also took him to countless museums and historical sites.

Because he was always moving, John spent very little time in school. But thanks to help from private tutors, John could read and write very well by the age of nine. He learned to speak French, German, and Italian by traveling to those countries. Along the way, he also learned Greek, Latin, math, and music.

As a young teenager, John received his first art lessons from a German American landscape painter named Carl Welsch. Later in his teens, John took a drawing class at the Florence Academy of Fine Arts. When he was eighteen, his family moved to Paris, France. There he entered the studio of Carolus-Duran, the leading portrait painter in Paris at that time. For the first time in his life, John was a full-time art student. He made the most of it, becoming one of the most celebrated portrait painters of his day.

JOHN
AT **14**

The Matterhorn
1870
Fogg Art Museum,
Cambridge,
Massachusetts

John drew constantly as a boy. When he was twelve, he began filling sketchbooks with scenes from his family's travels. When he was fourteen, John and his father took a three-week walking tour of the Swiss Alps. One of the sketches he made on that trip is this watercolor of the Matterhorn. It is one of the highest peaks in the Alps.

When he was sixteen, John's family spent a few months in Germany. While they were there, he made this pencil and charcoal sketch of a little German town called Engelsburg. It shows how skillful he was at shading and capturing different textures. For John, accuracy was always more important than originality in his drawings.

JOHN
AT**16**

Engelsburg
1872
British Museum,
London, England

18

Carnation, Lily, Lily, Rose
1885—1886
Tate Gallery,
London, England

This painting is one of John's best-loved works. It shows two girls lighting paper lanterns in a garden. He was trying to capture a brief time of evening, when the yellow lanterns started to outshine the purple twilight. This effect lasted for about twenty minutes each day. As a result, the painting took John two summers to complete, when he was twenty-nine and thirty.

PAULKLEE
(December 18, 1879–June 29, 1940)

Did you know that when Paul Klee was bored in class, he liked to draw in his schoolbooks?

Paul Klee was one of the most original artists of the twentieth century. Using his sense of humor, his love for music, and his interest in looking at things like a child does, he developed a very playful approach to creating art.

Paul was born near Bern, Switzerland. His grandmother introduced him to drawing and coloring. She gave Paul paper, crayons, and scissors at a very young age. She also painted little pictures for him. She even read him fairy tales to jump-start his imagination.

Paul always had a strong imagination. Even at the age of three or four, he was making drawings of the "evil spirits" that he dreamed about. Sometimes he copied pictures from a local calendar. It was illustrated with landscape paintings of Bern, where he grew up.

According to his sister, Mathilde, Paul drew with his left hand and wrote with his right hand. He could also draw and write with both hands at the same time. He could go from left to right or from right to left.

Paul was a good student, but he often drew in his schoolbooks. While he pretended to listen to his teachers, he filled the margins with fantastic or funny drawings. By the time he was sixteen, Paul was drawing detailed landscapes that were very advanced for his age.

Paul's other great interest as a boy was music. His father was a music teacher, and his mother was a trained pianist and singer. So it was no surprise when Paul started playing the violin at the age of seven. When he was eleven, he was chosen as an extra for the Municipal Orchestra of Bern. At the age of eighteen, Paul had to decide between music and art. He chose to study art in Munich, Germany. It was a decision he never regretted.

Untitled (Merry-go-round)
ca. 1889
Zentrum Paul Klee,
Bern, Switzerland

This is Paul's drawing of the carousel in his hometown. He made it when he was ten. Paul first learned how to draw from his grandmother. He drew with his left hand, which bothered one of his aunts. When she suggested that Paul should use his right hand, his grandmother replied, "The child will use the hand he feels he can use better."

As a teenager, Paul could draw quite realistically. In this pen and ink drawing, he captured his boyhood bedroom in amazing detail. He was sixteen. But as Paul got older, he became less interested in drawing what he saw. He was more interested in using lines, shapes, and colors to capture thoughts from his own imagination.

PAUL AT**16**

My Room
1896
Zentrum Paul Klee,
Bern, Switzerland

Cat and Bird
1928
The Museum of Modern Art,
New York

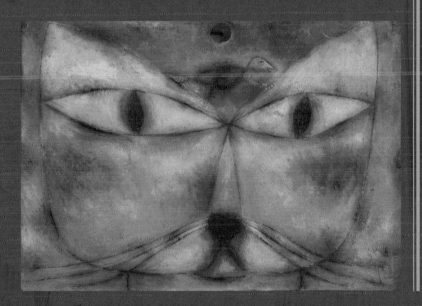

The cat was Paul's favorite animal. He made this childlike painting when he was forty-nine. With just a few simple lines, Paul shows us both the cat and what the cat is thinking about— a bird. Also notice the red heart for the cat's nose. Even when Paul was an adult, he wanted to paint like a child. He loved how creative children could be without even thinking about it.

PABLO PICASSO
(October 25, 1881–April 8, 1973)

Did you know that when Pablo Picasso was young, he often chose to draw instead of playing with his friends?

Pablo Picasso is best known as the inventor of cubism. But he was an artist of many styles. His parents saved much of his childhood artwork. They believed that Pablo would become a great artist someday. They were right. Pablo became the most famous artist of the twentieth century.

Pablo was born in Malaga, Spain. According to his mother, Pablo could draw before he could speak. His first word was *piz*. This is short for *lapiz*, the Spanish word for "pencil." His father was a painter, a museum curator, and an art teacher. So naturally, he became Pablo's first art teacher.

As a young boy, Pablo drew all the time. He even preferred drawing to playing with his friends. For fun, his cousins or sisters would ask him to draw something, like a donkey. But they would tell him to start at the ear or some other part of the body. Pablo could always do it. He also amazed them with lifelike paper cutouts of dogs, roosters, and other animals.

As his first teacher, Pablo's father taught him the traditional rules of art. But as Pablo got older, he became impatient with these rules. He wanted to try new things. By the time Pablo was thirteen, his father realized that his son was a better artist than he was. So he gave Pablo his paints and brushes and declared he would never paint again.

When Pablo was sixteen, his father sent him to art school in Madrid, Spain's capital. But Pablo didn't like it. He often skipped school and went to the Prado, Madrid's famous art museum. There he studied the work of earlier Spanish artists like Diego Velázquez, Francisco de Goya, and El Greco.

After a few months in Madrid, Pablo returned home. He started spending time with other artists, who told him that Paris was the center of modern art. The more they talked, the more Pablo wanted to go. So at the age of eighteen, Pablo packed his bags for Paris. It was here that a few years later, he changed the course of modern art.

Little Picador
1890
Private Collection,
Málaga, Spain

Pablo's father often took him to bullfights when he was young. Pablo loved the bullfights. He and his friends spent hours pretending to be matadors. Pablo painted this scene from a bullfight, called *Little Picador*, when he was just eight years old. The picador is a man on horseback who wears down the bull before the matador performs.

PABLO AT 15

Self-Portrait

1896

Museu Picasso,
Barcelona, Spain

When Pablo was thirteen, his family moved to Barcelona. He went to art school there with students who were five and six years older than he was. But as an artist, he was ahead of them all. By the time he was sixteen, Pablo had his own studio. He had also created two major paintings. He painted this confident self-portrait when he was fifteen.

When he was about twenty-six, Pablo began developing a new art style called cubism. In cubism, the artist uses his or her imagination to "take apart" the object being painted and then "reassembles" it on the canvas. The idea is to show the object from many different angles, all at once. Pablo painted this cubist portrait of his first art dealer, Ambroise Vollard, when he was twenty-eight.

SALVADORDALÍ

(May 11, 1904–January 23, 1989)

Did you know that when Salvador Dalí was about ten, his father let him turn their laundry room into a painting studio?

As a boy, Salvador was spoiled by his parents. Their first son died before Salvador was born, so they wanted to make sure their second son was healthy and happy. Of course, they had no idea he would grow up to become one of the world's most famous artists. Today, when most people hear the word *surrealism*, they think of Salvador Dalí.

Salvador often said that he started drawing when he was a baby. But he often exaggerated the truth to get attention. According to his sister, Anna Maria, some of Salvador's first drawings were done on the balcony of their childhood apartment. On this balcony, there was a red table. Salvador made pictures of swans and ducks by scratching into the table's red paint, revealing the white surface underneath.

Salvador's parents were not very artistic. But Salvador remembered his mother creating little books for him and his sister. She drew animals on long strips of paper and then folded the strips like an accordion. She was always very supportive of his art.

Salvador's father was a notary, someone who writes contracts and witnesses signatures. However, he gave Salvador one of his greatest childhood inspirations—a complete set of Gowans's art books.

Each of these books contained sixty paintings by a great master of European art. There were fifty-two volumes in all, containing 3,120 works of art. Salvador spent endless hours looking at these books. By the time he was ten, he knew all the paintings by heart. From these, he learned what art could be.

When Salvador was nine or ten, his father allowed him to set up a studio in the laundry room of their apartment. Here Salvador read his art books, practiced drawing and painting, and dreamed of becoming a famous artist. By the time he was thirteen, his father was exhibiting Salvador's work in their home. At eighteen Salvador went off to art school in Madrid, where he began attracting the attention of the rest of the world.

Landscape
ca. 1910—1914
Salvador Dali Museum,
Saint Petersburg, Florida

Salvador always claimed he did this painting when he was six years old. But he was probably closer to ten or eleven. Salvador painted it over an old postcard. You can see the postcard lines under the paint. Figueras is the town in Spain where Salvador grew up. The snow-covered mountain in the background is Canigou, part of the Pyrenees mountain range.

SALVADOR
AT 14

Self-Portrait

ca. 1918–1919

Salvador Dalí Museum,
Saint Petersburg, Florida

This is Salvador's first known self-portrait. He painted it in Cadaques, Spain, when he was about fourteen. Cadaques is a popular vacation area, where Salvador spent many summers as a boy. In this painting, Salvador was experimenting with the loose brushstrokes and bright colors of impressionism. This is a sketchy painting style used to capture a quick impression of something.

Here is one of the most famous paintings in the history of art. Salvador painted it when he was twenty-seven. By this time, he had tried many styles. He finally settled on surrealism, a style based on dreams and thoughts from the subconscious mind. According to Salvador, the idea for the soft watches came to him one night after he ate some soft Camembert cheese.

Photo Acknowledgments

Cover art courtesy of: © 2010 Artists Rights Society (ARS), New York/VG Bild-Kunst, Bonn, Paul Klee, *Ohne Titel (Karussell)*, um 1889, *Untitled (Merry-go-round)*, pencil on paper, 11 x 14,1 cm, Privatbesitz Schweiz, Depositum im Zentrum Paul Klee, Bern (top left); Paul Klee, 1892, Foto: M. Vollenweider & Sohn, Bern, 10,5 x 6,4 cm, Zentrum Paul Klee, Bern, Schenkung Familie Klee (top right); © 2010 Estate of Pablo Picasso/Artists Rights Society (ARS), New York, Photograph © Art Resource, NY (bottom left); © Apic/Hulton Archive/Getty Images (bottom right).

Interior art courtesy of: Page 4: © Bildarchiv Preussischer Kulturbesitz/Art Resource, NY; Page 5: Graphische Sammlung Albertina, Vienna, Austria/The Bridgeman Art Library; Page 6: © Scala/Ministero per i Beni e le Attività culturali/Art Resource, NY; Page 7: Graphische Sammlung Albertina, Vienna, Austria/The Bridgeman Art Library; Page 8: © Erich Lessing/Art Resource, NY; Page 9: Michelangelo Buonarroti, *The Torment of Saint Anthony*, ca. 1487-88, Oil and tempera on panel, 18 1/2 x 13 3/4 in. © Kimbell Art Museum, Fort Worth, Texas/Art Resource, NY; Page 10: © Scala/Art Resource, NY; Page 11: © SuperStock/SuperStock; Page 12: © akg-images; Page 13: © Scala/Ministero per i Beni e le Attività culturali/Art Resource, NY; Page 14: © Scala/Ministero per i Beni e le Attivitá culturali/Art Resource, NY; Page 15: The Royal Collection © 2010, Her Majesty Queen Elizabeth II; Page 16: © Tate, London/Art Resource, NY; Page 17: John Singer Sargent, *The Matterhorn*, 1870, Watercolor and graphite on off-white wove paper, actual: 38.8 x 27 cm (15 1/4 x 10 5/8 in.) Harvard Art Museum, Fogg Art Museum, Gift of Mrs. Francis Ormond, 1937.2, Photo: Katya Kallsen © President and Fellows of Harvard College; Page 18–19: © The Trustees of the British Museum/Art Resource, NY; Page 19: © Tate, London/Art Resource, NY; Page 20: Paul Klee, 1892, Foto: M. Vollenweider & Sohn, Bern, 10,5 x 6,4 cm, Zentrum Paul Klee, Bern, Schenkung Familie Klee; Page 21: © 2010 Artists Rights Society (ARS), New York/VG Bild-Kunst, Bonn, Paul Klee, *Ohne Titel (Karussell)*, um 1889, *Untitled (Merry-go-round)*, pencil on paper, 11 x 14,1 cm, Privatbesitz Schweiz, Depositum im Zentrum Paul Klee, Bern; Page 22–23: © 2010 Artists Rights Society (ARS), New York/VG Bild-Kunst, Bonn, Paul Klee, *Meine Bude*, 1896, *My Pad*, pen, brush and pencil on paper, 12,1 x 19,2 cm, Zentrum Paul Klee, Bern; Page 23: © 2010 Artists Rights Society (ARS), New York/VG Bild-Kunst, Bonn, Paul Klee, *Cat and Bird*, 1928, Oil and ink on gessoed canvas, mounted on wood, 15 x 21" (38.1 x 53.2 cm), Sidney and Harriet Janis Collection Fund, and gift of Suzy Prudden and Joan H. Meijer in memory of F. H. Hirschland (300.1975), Digital Image © The Museum of Modern Art/Licensed by Scala/Art Resource, NY; Page 24: © Apic/Hulton Archive/Getty Images; Page 25: © 2010 Estate of Pablo Picasso/Artists Rights Society (ARS), New York, Photograph © Art Resource, NY; Page 26: © 2010 Estate of Pablo Picasso/Artists Rights Society (ARS), New York, Museu Picasso, Barcelona, Spain/The Bridgeman Art Library; Page 27: © 2010 Estate of Pablo Picasso/Artists Rights Society (ARS), New York, Photograph © Scala/Art Resource, NY; Page 28: Rue des Archives/The Granger Collection, New York; Page 29: *Landscape* (1910-14) Oil on cardboard, 14 x 9 cm, © 2010 Salvador Dali, Gala-Salvador Dali Foundation/Artist Rights Society (ARS), New York, Collection of the Salvador Dalí Museum, Inc., St. Petersburg, FL, 2010; Page 30: *Self-portrait* (1918-19) Oil on canvas, 10 1/2 x 8 1/4 inches, © 2010 Salvador Dali, Gala-Salvador Dali Foundation/Artist Rights Society (ARS), New York, Collection of the Salvador Dalí Museum, Inc., St. Petersburg, FL, 2010; Page 30–31: © 2010 Salvador Dali, Gala-Salvador Dali Foundation /Artist Rights Society (ARS), New York, Salvador Dalí, *The Persistence of Memory*, 1931, Oil on canvas, 9 1/2 x 13" (24.1 x 33 cm), given anonymously (162.1934), Digital Image © The Museum of Modern Art/Licensed by Scala/Art Resource, NY.